INK: A Life in Letters

INK: A Life in Letters

Joe Junod

ISBN-13: 9781523949861
ISBN-10: 1523949864
Library of Congress Control Number: 2016902446
CreateSpace Independent Publishing Platform
North Charleston, South Carolina

For my wife, Marilyn Greene,
an outstanding journalist and
the love of my life.

Plaudits

"In *Ink: A Life in Letters*, veteran newspaper editor Joe Junod presents a compendium of the experiences and ideas that shaped his career, life, and thinking. Assembled alphabetically like a well-worn Rolodex on a newspaper reporter's desk, Junod's take on topics from attitude to zest are pearls of wisdom. A pleasure to read, dotted with thoughtful aphorisms, *Ink* will leave you with lot to think about." - James McGrath Morris, author of *Pulitzer: A Life in Politics, Print, and Power*

"This is a delightful easy read. Junod is at his best when he writes about his personal experiences, people he has known and worked with, people who have taught him real life lessons. These gems make INK: A Life in Letters worth your time" - Jeffrey Packard, Episcopal priest

"Cheers to Joe Junod. His book provides professional, personal and philosophical insight and advice from which any reader can benefit. This is a strong read with even stronger lessons for the reader." - Phil Currie, retired newspaper executive

Preface

By Blair Turner,
Professor of History,
Virginia Military Institute

WE'LL START WITH A LITTLE journalistic name dropping before I get to Joe's story. A couple years back, I had the pleasure of participating in a seminar for a few days with the best-selling journalist-writer, Robert Kaplan, at a neighboring, venerable university in the Commonwealth of Virginia (colors are blue and white, nickname the "Generals").

Kaplan was back from one of his globe-trotting jaunts and we all got together to read some stuff on global problems in the Middle East or some such place. The geographic niceties weren't what was important. His message was, and it has stuck with me. Just look and write what you see: observe and report. Kaplan said he knew he would never be able to see all the angles of any story—he'd never be able to "get it right." That would take lots of different stories and then more historians to sort them all out. But, what he could do was exercise keenness of eye and craft of language to at least let the rest of us see something, feel some truth. I've never forgotten his analysis of the reporter's job. Apparently, Joe knew that early on and has been following the path all along.

He was editor of the college newspaper at the small liberal arts school we attended in North Carolina. I think I even wrote a sports story or two for him back then, but maybe not; too long ago, can't recall. We were pretty smart in those days and both graduated with honors in 1969.

After college, Joe got 4-F'd and went off to a career in newspapering. I got an all-expenses paid trip to Southeast Asia courtesy of Uncle Sam. By the time I got back, he was a full-fledged reporter for *The Salisbury Post*, in North Carolina. You might think Salisbury is a small place, and it is, but it's not Mayberry. The *Post* is more than a century old, and the city is headquarters of the Food Lion chain and the home of - that's right - *Cheerwine*. Not only that, Salisbury was reputed to boast more millionaires per capita (see Food Lion) that any town in America.

Joe may have had to spend time studying sowbelly price trends there, but he was also learning how to report. When Stevie Wonder's entourage cruised into a pile-up on the interstate near Salisbury one day, Joe was the man on the spot to cover the story and nail down the hard facts like the one that Stevie wasn't the one driving. What is it about North Carolina and writers and journalists? Newspaperman Tom Wicker came from Hamlet—appropriately named, smaller than Salisbury. Anchorman and author David Brinkley and novelist Robert Ruark were from Wilmington. Something to that, I think. Anyway, by the time he left, Joe could write.

Good enough, anyhow, for him to go to Florida to be an editor on *The Fort Myers News-Press*. We saw a lot of Joe in those days because my wife and I were at the University of Florida in Gainesville, chasing a career of permanent poverty in academia. Joe would drive up for refreshment and renewal. But it wasn't all fun and games; he was still doing his job and learning his craft pretty well, it would seem, because he wound up as managing editor of *The Ithaca Journal* in New York by the end of the '70's.

There he made his biggest career and life move and married the wonderful Miss Marilyn. We were there for the wedding. Smartest thing he ever did aside from getting me to write this. She is a journalist, too - and a dear friend. In 1981, *The Journal* was named Gannett's top ranked newspaper. Not too long after, Joe fleeted up to corporate and the big bucks. I recall that one of his perks was a car. No beamer for Joe; he got a truck; big thing; he played Elvis singing gospel on the CD.

This is my friend of some 50 years. He has been observing and reporting all along and it all comes together in these pages you have in front of you. It's not "the right story," but it is the story of the right people and what Joe has learned from them. Lots of stories. In them:

- ● an editor of the Southern town's newspaper bucks the system and refuses to give "Negro News" second fiddle;
- ● a captain of industry saves lives by creating and endowing the Sloan-Kettering Cancer Center;
- ● a custodial worker's steady, silent dignity inspires generations;
- ● a journalism magnate's only regret after decades of success turns out to be losing the free rides on his beloved corporate jet;
- ● a reporter stares down a pistol-waving KKK-er and gets the picture for the newspaper, too!
- ● a survivor of the Nazi death camps teaches Joe a lesson in honor;
- ● and, there was a car dealer in the Bronx named *Mickey Lipp* (I'm not making this up).
- ● Not to mention the cameo appearances by the Wright Brothers, C.S. Lewis, William Faulkner, Rogers & Hammerstein and many more names than I can drop. The characters are inspirations *from* and *for* a real life, captured in clear, easy prose. Think Studs Terkel or Jimmy Breslin.

You're going to enjoy this.

Introduction

It was, as they say, the ride of a lifetime. I wouldn't trade it for a mint Mickey Mantle rookie card.

Four decades in the newspaper busi-ness can do many nasty things to even the sanest person: kill you, drive you to drink, or turn you into a cynical observer of the human race.

Fortunately, I dodged those bullets, as my years in the trade exposed me to a nonstop wonderland of people, expe-riences, and ideas. A few of those peo-ple, experiences, and ideas were nasty, unpleasant, and dumb. But they repre-sent the minority.

Mickey Mantle

Using the alphabet as my guide, I present here a few of those fine people, experiences, and ideas that shaped my career, my life, and my thinking.

Attitude

Some say attitude is everything in life. It is who you are. Others say attitude is just a posture, a pose without meaning.

The word can be used as a positive (Now that's the attitude!) or as a negative (What's with the snarky attitude, buster?).

The dictionary offers multiple definitions, but only two are of interest to me. One definition is that attitude is a position assumed to serve a purpose. The second says attitude is a behavior representing a feeling or conviction. I like the second because for me attitude is part of our nature. The first definition is not incorrect; it just seems less profound than the second.

The word is a powerful one, as is attitude itself.

Think of some famous people who have distinctive attitudes:

- President George W. Bush, a certain swagger
- Baseball great Cal Ripken, a certain humility
- TV star Oprah Winfrey, a certain curiosity
- Media CEO Al Neuharth, a certain determination (see letter W)
- Baseball great Henry Aaron, a certain grace

It has been my experience that people living fulfilling lives view the world as a glass half-full and greet the morning with eagerness. Their attitudes are not about themselves but are directed outward—to achievement, to others, and to service. For me, that's the right attitude, the essence of success.

Oprah Winfrey

In my four decades as a journalist and media executive, I saw many examples of attitude at work: positive attitudes producing excellent work and teamwork and negative attitudes producing mediocre work and workplace chaos. Attitude is a powerful tool, for good or ill.

The best reporters and editors I knew had attitude…an attitude to get the story first, get it right, and get it on time.

The worst reporters and editors I knew had another kind of attitude: selfish, lazy, and uninterested in developing their skills. One young reporter was working the night police beat when I was running the city desk at a Florida newspaper. The police squawk box belched out a fire alarm, and the kid just sat there, ignoring it. I told him to get going. He said, "I can't; I'm working on an investigative series." I basically kicked his butt out the door. The next morning, I charged into the editor's office and told him to fire the lazy-ass reporter.

The editor smiled and pulled down an annual report. Flipping to the pages featuring the board of directors, he pointed to one. "That's his father. No can do. But stay on him. Maybe he'll learn something." The kid never changed. It was sad.

Here's an insightful commentary on attitude by written by Charles Swindoll, a contemporary minister, in the late 20th century:

> The longer I live, the more I realize the impact of attitude on life. Attitude, to me, is more important than facts. It is more important than the past, than education, than money, than circumstances, than failures, than successes, than what other people think or say or do. It is more important than appearances, giftedness, or skill. It will make or break a company, a church, and a home.

The remarkable thing is we have a choice every day regarding the attitude we will embrace for that day. We cannot change our past. We cannot change the fact that people will act in a certain way. We cannot change the inevitable. The only thing we can do is play on the one string we have, and that is our attitude.

I am convinced that life is 10 percent what happens to me and 90 percent how I react to it. And so it is with you. We are in charge of our attitudes.

Philosopher Henry James summed up the business of attitude another way: "The greatest discovery of our generation is that human beings can alter their lives by altering their attitudes of mind. As you think, so shall you be."

Balance

WE STRIVE TO FIND BALANCE in life: between work and home, between spending and saving, between faith and science.

In journalism, we strive to report all sides of an issue. Sometimes we fail, but most times we get the balance right. Balanced reporting and editing generates trust among readers and sources.

In the corporate world, platitudes abounded when the word "balance" was the topic.

My two favorite corporate platitudes are the following:

1. Our employees are our most important asset.
2. Proper work-life balance is very important to this company.

Regarding the first platitude, I have observed more managers and executives who used this phrase and then acted in the opposite manner than those whose actions reflected their belief in the adage. One particular trait in managers whose actions refute this adage is common: "Suck up; beat down."

As a young man, I worked for an editor who thought little of me and made my work life miserable on more days than I care to count. All that joy for $135 a week and no health insurance! But my work life improved after my college Shakespeare professor James Carver—a saint!—suggested that I study my boss's behavior as a

learning experience in preparation for becoming a manager and leader myself. It worked.

Here's an example. This guy loved to upbraid staff in public, often profanely. (I wasn't his only target.) Before I ever heard the admonition "praise in public, criticize in private," I knew it was the right thing to do because it was what this guy didn't do.

Although I can offer no proof to substantiate the following theory, I am convinced it is valid: the higher the rank of the executive mouthing platitudes, the less sincere he or she is.

But let's return to the subject of work-life balance.

My wife, Marilyn, and I have lived for three decades in a suburb of Washington, DC. I don't believe there is another place in the country where the concept of work-life balance is more out of whack than in DC. I have seen a T-shirt emblazoned with this: "Washington, DC. Ten square miles surrounded by reality." Have truer words ever been printed or spoken?

There are basically six tribes in DC:

1. Politicians and public servants
2. Attorneys, lobbyists, and consultants
3. The media
4. The military
5. The medical profession
6. Everyone else

Tribes one through five are populated with flocks of folks who typically get to work early and get home late. I knew one guy with small children who left the house before the kids got up and usually got home after they were asleep. Plus, he had a ninety-minute commute each way—that is, ninety minutes on a good traffic day, and in the DC area, those days are rare. There's no need to tell you what happened to his marriage.

In my experience, folks in tribe six come closer to a decent work-life balance than other tribes. In other words, teachers, cops, firefighters, service techs, carpenters, hairdressers, and their ilk do something besides work. And they think about something besides work, salary, career, and promotion. Full disclosure: for more years than I care to count, I was a happy and devoted part of tribe three, and my life and my work were not always in balance. Newspapering can disrupt the balance rapidly because reporting and editing the news are so often soul consuming.

Charles de Gaulle is said to have remarked, "The graveyards are full of indispensable men." And women. Such wisdom.

Former defense secretary Bob Gates strikes me as one of those rare birds who understands how intoxicating a place Washington, DC, can become for so many people.

A few years ago, he told the Marine Memorial Association, "It's a pleasure to be with you in San Francisco, but then I have to confess, it's a pleasure to be anywhere but Washington, DC, a place where so many people are lost in thought because it's such unfamiliar territory. Where people say, 'I'll double-cross that bridge when I get to it.' The only place in the world you can see a prominent person walking down Lover's Lane holding his own hand."

Bob Gates

Here's a final thought: you never hear the phrase spoken or written as "life-work balance." What does that tell you about its sincerity?

Creativity

THE COMMON UNDERSTANDING OF THIS word applies to the use of the imagination to create art—sculpture, fiction, painting, and theater.

That's too narrow a definition for my taste. Rather, we see and experience an abundance of creativity around us every day. We can see it in products, services, procedures, and policies.

Take the automobile. Creativity pours out of cars today: GPS, audio enhancements, and safety improvements are just for starters. Most of us don't see, much less understand, the creativity that goes into improving safety and gas mileage, reducing pollution, and extending the life of the car.

Take medical advances. Most of us have witnessed the rapid improvement in medications, equipment, and surgical procedures. Here's one small example: gall-bladder surgery. When my mother had her gall bladder removed years ago, a long incision was made in her abdomen. Her stomach muscles took months to heal. It was a painful and lengthy experience. Today a small incision—less than an inch—is made in the belly button. The patient goes home after surgery, and recovery time is minimal.

What about statins to fight cholesterol and heart disease? How many lives have been lengthened by the creativity of medical scientists? Would my father have lived longer than sixty-four years if he'd had statins? I suspect so. My doctor and I were talking about medical advances, and he said the greatest advance in his career was Lipitor. Before statins hit the market, Doc said he'd have fifty to seventy-five patients a year requiring some form of cardiovascular surgery. Today he has but one or two.

Consider the media creativity unleashed by the Internet. News websites—whether run by establishment media like newspapers or by newcomers—abound with creativity and interactivity. For me, the Internet has enhanced press freedom by providing a wider and deeper platform for more voices to be heard. Yes, some of those voices are unbalanced and dangerous, but here the benefits far outweigh the negatives.

John Metzger was perhaps the most creative journalist I ever worked with. He reported with a camera, and oh, how he did report. His eye, his sense of timing, and his handiwork in the darkroom (remember those?) were unmatched in my experience. John believed that it was his mission to produce photographs that evoked emotion and told worthy stories to his readers. After his too-early death,

Charles Kettering

another legacy emerged. Dozens of photographers whom John had nurtured at newspapers across the country spoke of John's guidance and the extent to which he had boosted their careers and skills.

One of my favorite creative minds was Charles Kettering (1876–1958). In the first half of the twentieth century, Kettering was, to use a word wrongly applied to many, a titan—a creative industrial entrepreneur of the highest order. Unlike other geniuses, such as Thomas Edison and Steve Jobs, Kettering is little known or appreciated today. But in his time, he went on a decades-long creative tear.

In no particular order, Kettering invented

* the electric starter, ignition, and lighting systems for cars;
* leaded gasoline;

- Freon for refrigeration and air conditioning;
- the first color enamels for painting cars;
- an incubator for premature babies; and
- a generator known as a Delco plant that electrified farms outside the electric grid.

Plus, he had the first air-conditioned house in the country, if not the world.

There's much more, but my favorite is the aerial torpedo he invented in 1918. The Kettering Bug was made of papier-mâché, with twelve-foot cardboard wings. It could carry three hundred pounds of explosives at fifty miles per hour. The Bug is considered by many to be the first aerial missile. It led to the development of guided missiles.

Kettering has a town, a university, and numerous schools named after him. He and his partner at General Motors, Albert Sloan, used their wealth to found the Memorial Sloan Kettering Cancer Center. Kettering was a man of high accomplishment who used his good fortune and his keen mind to help many others across generations.

Kettering is also the author of memorable one-liners. Here are a few:

- "The Wright brothers flew right through the smoke screen of impossibility."
- "An inventor is simply a fellow who doesn't take his education too seriously."
- "A person must have a certain amount of intelligent ignorance to get anywhere."
- "There is a great difference between knowing and understanding: You can know a lot about something and not really understand it. You can be sincere and still be stupid."
- "A problem well stated is a problem half solved."

Kettering has taught me much, especially about lifelong learning and perseverance.

Another favorite creator of mine is William Shakespeare. Oh, I admire the majesty of his sonnets (the twenty-fifth is my favorite) and his plays (*Henry V* is my favorite.) But when one examines the words and phrases he coined, astonishment is the only response.

In all his works, Shakespeare used 17,677 words at least once, according to scholars. Of those, he created—or adapted from other languages—1,700. Add to that dozens and dozens of phrases he created that we regularly use, such as "heart of gold" (*Henry V*), "brave new world" (*The Tempest*), "in my mind's eye" (*Hamlet*), and "neither rhyme nor reason" (*As You Like It*).

William Shakespeare

Author Bernard Levin parsed this delightful romp through Shakespeare's impact on our language:

If you cannot understand my argument, and declare "It's Greek to me," you are quoting Shakespeare; if you claim to be more sinned against than sinning, you are quoting Shakespeare; if you recall your salad days, you are quoting Shakespeare; if you act more in sorrow than in anger, if your wish is father to the thought, if your lost property has vanished into thin air, you are quoting Shakespeare; if you have ever refused to budge an inch or suffered from green-eyed jealousy, if you have played fast and loose, if you have been tongue-tied, a tower of strength, hoodwinked or in a pickle, if you have knitted your brows, made a virtue of necessity, insisted on fair play, slept not one wink, stood on ceremony, danced attendance (on your lord and master), laughed yourself into stitches, had short shrift, cold comfort or too much of a good thing, if you have seen better days or lived in a fool's paradise—why, be that as it may, the more fool you, for it is a foregone conclusion that you are (as good luck would have it) quoting Shakespeare; if you think it is early days and clear out bag and baggage, if you think it is high time and that that is the long and short of it, if you believe that the game is up and that truth will out even if it involves your own flesh and blood, if you lie low till the crack of doom because you suspect foul play, if you have your teeth set on edge (at one fell swoop) without rhyme or reason, then—to give the devil his due—if the truth were known (for surely you have a tongue in your head) you are quoting Shakespeare; even if you bid me good riddance and send me packing, if you wish I were dead as a door-nail, if you think I am an eyesore, a laughing stock, the devil incarnate, a stony-hearted villain, bloody-minded or a blinking idiot, then—by Jove! O Lord! Tut, tut! for goodness' sake! what the dickens! but me no buts—it is all one to me, for you are quoting Shakespeare. (*The Story of English*, 145)

If you enjoy language and its origins, search for Shakespeare's words and phrases. You'll have a fine time.

A final story about the Bard. Some scholars believe Shakespeare was involved in the translation and editing of the Bible into the King James Version (KJV), a project that started in London in 1604. There is no proof that he did in fact work on the translation. But there remains the wording of Psalm 46. When the KJV was published in 1611, Shakespeare was around forty-six. (Scholars have never pinned down his birth date). In the KJV—and only in the KJV—you find these two words in Psalm 46: "shake" and "spear." Count forty-six words from the start, and you find "shake." Count forty-six words from the end, and you encounter "spear." A coincidence? Or a cosmic joke inserted by our greatest writer? Who knows? It is a great literary nugget.

Doing the Right Thing

Paul Miller

THE CEO OF GANNETT IN the 1960s and 1970s used the phrase "do the right thing" a lot. I don't suspect Paul Miller coined the phrase, but he repeatedly said that it guided his business and personal decisions. He urged executives and managers to follow that advice. Smart guy. I've learned over the years that this is a wise and just way to make decisions.

In encouraging folks to do the right thing, Miller was not equating the right thing with the easy thing, the quick thing, or the expedient thing. He was suggesting that we ask ourselves whether what we are about to do is the appropriate and ethical decision, given all the evidence we have at hand.

I believe that his use of "right" was not a synonym for "correct" but rather an embrace of values as a guiding light. The "right" thing can be a very hard thing to do.

When I realized I needed to fire my first staffer—a reporter—I was terrified. But I got good coaching from my boss (focus on the disruptive behavior, not the person; ensure the person's dignity is not damaged), and I took comfort in remembering to "do the right thing" because it meant we could create a more collegial newsroom.

This phrase came to mind when I was introduced to C. S. Lewis's interpretation of the Tao—a universal moral law that many thoughtful people have considered over the centuries. Lewis held that every tribe, every grouping of people from ancient times onward, devised a code—a code of conduct or behavior, if you will. His research can be found in the appendix of his book *The Abolition of Man*. His Tao is a supreme guide to moral and ethical values. The author of this moral code, says Lewis, is God.

C.S. Lewis

For Lewis, the Tao is proof of God's existence and his active role in the world. Here is Lewis's reasoning, as I understand it: If all these tribes, since the beginning of man, wrote a similar code of conduct, the author must be divine. How else can one explain the similarity of all these codes?

In another view of the concept, Kathryn Lindskoog and G. F. Ellwood wrote in a 1984 article in *Christian Century* that "the human race is haunted by the desire to do what is right. People invariably defend their actions by arguing that those actions do not really contradict a basic standard of behavior or that the standard was violated for good reasons."

Enterprise

THIS IS A MARVELOUS WORD. It conveys so much: energy, direction, enthusiasm, and thoughtfulness. (The noun can also mean a business, but that's not the point here.)

Enterprise is for me the best of all words for America, for it is enterprise that founded and enriched this country, built it, and nurtured it. Enterprise brought the Pilgrims; enterprise separated the colonies from the British; enterprise fueled the western migration; enterprise won the Civil War; and enterprise built steel yards, railroads, and highways. Enterprise gave us Poe, Melville, Dickinson, Edison, Hemingway, Steinbeck, Buck, and O'Neill. Enterprise ended World War II, put men on the moon, and, in the long process of development, made America the envy of the world.

Emily Dickinson

The United States isn't perfect by any means, but we do keep trying. Enterprise was and is the sublime American engine of progress.

The smartest newspaper editors, in my experience, value enterprise almost as much as accuracy and fairness. One of my editors, George Blake, believed that high-quality enterprise reporting is what separates OK news reports from outstanding news reports. In Blake's newsrooms, enterprise reporting was nonnegotiable.

Years ago in Ithaca, New York, a young reporter named John Maines quickly demonstrated to me that he had the enterprise gene—in spades. In 2013 the journalism world at large learned the same thing. John won the Pulitzer Gold Medal for reporting at the *Sun Sentinel* in Fort Lauderdale, Florida. When I heard the news, I was delighted but not surprised.

Here's one thing I believe all enterprising people share: dreams. And they chase those dreams with plans and guts and moxie. They instinctively know that dreams will never chase them.

Failure

_____

It TOOK ME A WHILE to figure this out, but failure can be very good for your soul—if you let it. If we open our minds and our emotions to it, failure can sharpen our wits, test our patience, and focus our activity. Failure can teach good lessons. I know because by any standard measure, I failed a lot growing up. In high school, I was awkward around girls, was lousy at sports, and, in four years, earned one B grade. (No, the rest were not As.) In retrospect, it is astonishing that I did not end up attending the University of Vietnam. (More on this in letter *H*).

From those high school days, I developed an enormous empathy for folks who struggle to achieve.

I have read with interest about parents and coaches who

Ted Turner

won't let their kids fail. Everyone plays. Everyone scores. Everyone gets a trophy. The fallacious argument is that failure at a young age damages self-esteem, and we can't let that happen, can we? But we should. Failure helps kids develop into well-rounded adults.

One of my favorite people is Ted Turner, founder of CNN. Of his many qualities, persistence stands out for me. Turner once told a reporter: "Why do you think my own racing yacht is named Tenacious? Because I never quit. I've got a bunch of flags on my boat, but there ain't no white flags. I don't surrender. That's the story of my life."

Genius

TED TURNER MIGHT BE ONE. He invented cable TV news. He did it the same year Al Neuharth created *USA Today*, in 1982. The entire media establishment ridiculed both ventures and both men. Guess who got the last laughs? (See letter *W* for more on Al.)

I've met folks who thought they were geniuses and told most everyone so. I even worked for one of these delusional people, for a very long thirty-two months and five days, but who's counting?

I know two geniuses—actually, musical savants. They will be none too pleased if they read this, as these are modest but enormously talented musicians.

Jack Williams

Singer-songwriter Jack Williams (www.jackwilliamsmusic.com) is one. Peter Yarrow of Peter, Paul, and Mary once wrote that Jack was, hands down, the best guitar player in America.

In one concert several years ago, a professional guitarist told me after Jack finished playing, "I couldn't keep up with him. What was he doing with that instrument?" Jack has been on the road for fifty-plus years, and he still brings his dazzling music, his great lyrics, and his delightful storytelling to deliver world-class performance art.

The second is a ragtime/boogie-woogie piano player Marilyn and I met a few years back at the Dixie Theatre in Apalachicola, Florida. His name is Bob Milne (www.bobmilne.com).

He has been touring for decades after years of playing ragtime piano in Detroit saloons. After a concert at our church in Spotsylvania Courthouse, Virginia, I asked Bob how many songs he knew. He thought for a minute and then shook his head and said, "I don't know." A few seconds later, Bob offered this: he suspected he could play one hundred two-hour concerts and never repeat a song. He taught himself the piano, doesn't read music, and never practices. But after hearing Bob for the first time, folks often wonder, Where were all the other musicians whose music I heard coming from the stage? Answer: There was none. Just Bob.

Bob Milne

Check Jack and Bob's websites for their tour schedules. You will not be disappointed if you attend one of their concerts, and you will have a memorable evening.

Other geniuses I have only observed at a distance. But we can see the results of genius in their creations. Four of the people who have helped change the trajectory of human development are Clarence Birdseye, Steve Jobs, and Orville and Wilbur Wright.

CLARENCE BIRDSEYE

All this gentleman did was change the way the world consumes food.

While working for the US Department of Agriculture in Labrador around 1912, he observed how Inuit fishermen flash froze their catch under ice. Instinctively, he knew this frozen fish was far superior in quality and taste

Clarence Birdseye

than the fish that was generally available in the States. Birdseye came home and devised methods of flash freezing fish and vegetables and getting them to market.

STEVE JOBS

Who besides Edison has created multiple lines of screamingly successful businesses? Steve Jobs.

Steve Jobs

In a commencement address some years ago, Jobs said, "I want to put a ding in the universe." Mac and iMac (ding), iPhone (ding), iPod (ding), and iPad (ding). Those are four dings. The last three were created when he returned to Apple after his board of directors had kicked him out because it had decided that Apple needed maturity and business experience. Well, remember what happened? Apple's fortunes sagged, and its stock got slammed after Jobs was shown the door.

Oh, I forgot about Pixar! That's five lines of famously great businesses. Five dings.

Who said there are no second acts?

THE WRIGHT BROTHERS

Orville and Wilbur's years of labor, observation, and glider testing resulted in humankind's first heavier-than-air powered and controlled flight on December 17, 1903, at Kitty Hawk, North Carolina.

Scholars believe that the brothers understood the four known forces of flight—lift (Bernoulli's principle), weight (gravity), thrust (Newton's second and third laws), and drag (a function of airspeed and lift)—and combined them with their own invention: the three-axis stabilizer.

By observing birds' flying motions and then testing their gliders, the brothers concluded that they could overcome the obstacle that had doomed earlier efforts by fully controlling the airplane through these mechanisms:

The Wright Brothers

- Pitch: the motion of the airplane as its nose points up or down. To control the pitch of their first glider, they used a wing mounted on the front of their glider. The Wrights called this wing their "front rudder."
- Roll: the tilting motion of the airplane around its longitudinal axis, which happens when one wing rises or falls in relation to the other. Wing warping was the method used by the Wrights to control roll. This process involves raising the front or leading edge of one side of the wing while dropping the leading edge of the other side of the wing.
- Yaw: the twisting motion around a plane's vertical axis as the nose turns left or right. Rudders control yaw. The force of air on a rudder deflected to the right causes the tail of the airplane to move to the left, which forces the nose to move to the right. (Information on the three-axis stabilizer can be found at www.investingflightschool.org.)

That three-axis system? It is still what enables all pilots to control their aircraft. Our youngest son, Patrick, was a Marine Corps fighter pilot, and the Wright brothers' insights and inventions still direct the F/A-18 and F-35 fighter jets he flew.

What's more, the brothers joined a stellar class of geniuses. Robert Q. Riley, an industrial designer and mechanical engineer, wrote the following on the one hundredth anniversary of the first flight:

The personal dimension of the Wright Brothers' conquest is equally as impressive as their technical achievement. Neither Orville nor Wilbur had graduated from high school (just like Edison and Ford). They had no formal training in the scientific theories and methodologies considered essential to designing a successful flying machine, so their chance of success was remote. As a result, they received no financial support. Their experiments had to be supported entirely with their own money...Not only did they conquer the air, they also conquered a world of skeptics and their own personal self-doubts. They accomplished what they should not have been able to accomplish.

We journalists are always on edge about missing the big story. Consider then what some might say is the biggest miss of the twentieth century. After their first successful flights, the brothers asked their family in Ohio to notify the press in Dayton. When informed that two local boys had just completed humankind's first powered flight, one that lasted fifty-seven seconds, Ohio Associated Press wire editor Frank Tunison retorted, "Fifty-seven seconds, hey? If it had been fifty-seven minutes, then it might have been a news item."

The Wrights, Birdseye and Jobs are rare cases. The business world is filled with very bright people who work hard and work well, and these leaders are regularly proclaimed to be geniuses. All this hero worship of business leaders is aided and abetted by the press. Witness the press's adoration of CEOs during the 1990s. How many of those cover-story faces are now in prison, dead, or in hiding?

Ken Lay, the ex-CEO of failed Enron, is the poster boy for false geniuses. He built a house of fantasy, and many investors and members of the media bought into it...and paid for it.

Two others deserve mention for their wit and their wisdom, as well as their contributions to the common good.

Mary Kay Ash was a genius. I had the good fortune some years ago to have lunch with three Mary Kay Ash saleswomen in Elmira, New York. For more than an hour, they talked about Mary Kay—not about cosmetics or their incomes but rather about how Mary Kay changed their lives and how she empowered them, and thousands

Mary Kay Ash

of other women, to improve themselves, their families, and their communities. When I asked if they considered Mary Kay a women's libber, they laughed and one said, "Absolutely. But she sure didn't look like one!"

Another genius was Peter Drucker. His writings are filled with insights about commerce and human nature.

Here is a favorite of mine. Business leaders are almost universally wrong about their primary goal, Drucker claimed. They think their primary goal is to make a profit, especially a profit that increases year after year.

Wrong, Drucker said. The principal goal is to make shoes. Make them well, market them well, and manage your internal business well, and the *result* will be profit.

For Drucker, profit was simply the result of manufacturing something or serving someone exceptionally well.

Handicaps

No, THIS IS NOT ABOUT golf.

It's about a word—"handicapped," as in crippled.

The word "handicapped" used to be considered more socially acceptable than "crippled." But even "handicapped" was later booted to the graveyard of hostile words and replaced with "disabled" by the word police. Later, other terms became part of our lexicon: special needs, differently abled, and mobility deficit. You can say this about the word police: they never rest in their attempts to sanitize the language and disguise the truth.

My introduction to folks in wheelchairs—or "wheelies," as they called themselves—came when I started college. My life until then had been, shall we say, sheltered. But that cocoon of safety was unraveling in the spring of my senior year in high school. The reason is that I was a lousy student, as I explained in letter *F* for failure. Not surprisingly, I was turned down by every college to which I applied, and Vietnam loomed as my next port of call.

A man named Roger Decker changed all that, and as a consequence, he altered the arc of my life and my future. He was in New York trawling for students for a fairly new college in North Carolina. He happened to stop by my high school, and he happened to chat with the one guidance counselor who knew something about me. Happenstance is the handmaiden of opportunity.

So on September 6, 1965, I flew to Charlotte with a duffel bag…and missed the last bus to Laurinburg, home of St. Andrews

Presbyterian College. I had thirty-three dollars on me, enough to satisfy one cabbie to drive the ninety-three miles to the place where I would spend four years learning how to think things through and to love the language and where I would grow up a whole lot.

Instantly, I was in a world I had never experienced before: the South of the midsixties. Water fountains and movie theaters still segregated white from black. When three of us (all New Yorkers) went to the Gibson Theater for the first time, "colored" patrons were directed to the balcony by a door on the street. So that's where the three of us went. We were soon booted from the theater. When we demanded our money back, the guy laughed at us and said something nasty about Yankees.

I learned that many southern college men were damned serious about clothing (I was not). They starched their shirts and emblazoned those shirts, as well as their sweaters and socks, with their monograms. One classmate must have had twenty alpaca sweaters of various colors, all with matching socks and all with monograms, of course. Folks dropped peanuts into their Pepsi or Cheerwine. They ate pigs' knuckles as if they were pickles.

The Presbyterians who founded St. Andrews in 1960 decided that it was their mission to build a campus accessible to everyone. So decades before a national awareness took hold, these folks built dorms and classrooms with sliding doors and wide doorjambs. Handicapped students had bedrooms on the first floor and assistance with bathing and dressing. Another amazing thing in retrospect is that they were not hustled off to separate classrooms. We were all in the same educational pot, long before the world discovered "mainstreaming."

My hat is off to the founders. Their vision taught me and, I am sure, many others about how we are, indeed, our brothers' and sisters' keepers.

Of course, I was totally intimidated by the handicapped students. I wouldn't talk to them, wouldn't look them in the eye, and absolutely would not sit next to them in class. In other words, I was normal, as we are instinctively offended or frightened by what is not like us.

That condition continued for maybe a month. It didn't last because several things became obvious: the wheelies (and those on crutches) didn't dwell in self-pity and were thrilled to be on campus. Most important, we learned that they shared the same passions and fears we all did.

One classmate, Carol White, could move only part of her upper body and was confined to an electric wheelchair. She was the class valedictorian and later became a dean at the University of California. When I received a B plus on an ethics paper from the fearsome philosophy professor Spencer Ludlow, I challenged him: "Why didn't I get an A?"

Spencer said, "The only people who get As from me are as smart as I am...and you are not." However, Carol got nothing but As from Spencer.

Integrity

I think of Jimmy Hurley, editor, publisher, and owner of the North Carolina–based *Salisbury Post* when I worked there in the 1970s.

In the 1960s, Hurley, a man raised in the Jim Crow South, made two changes that angered readers of all stripes...the rich, the not so rich, the powerful, and the powerless.

He decided his newspaper could no longer publish two-column-wide engagement and wedding photos of white women and one-column-wide photos of black women. So all such photos became one column wide. The white community, as you might expect, went nuts.

Jimmy Hurley

The second action was to eliminate the "Negro News" header in social news. All social news—white and black—would be published together. Well, the white community went crazy again, but Hurley was blindsided when a delegation of blacks came to his office and asked him to restore the "Negro News" header. Their fear was that black social news would be tagged onto the end of white social news and that if there was too much news for the available space, black news would be cut.

Hurley promised that would not happen. To the best of my knowledge, it didn't.

Through the uproar, Hurley listened, but he did not back down. That's integrity, backbone—and doing the right thing.

Journalism

EARLY ON, I WAS PRIVILEGED to learn the newspaper trade from very talented folks.

Joe Collins hired me over the telephone to be a reporter at the *Elk Valley Times*, a weekly in Fayetteville, Tennessee. Based on my voice and accent, he thought I was a black dude from New York City.

Over the next eighteen months, I learned the craft in a six-(sometimes seven) day-a-week cauldron of high expectations. Collins knew how to build a story, how to put the most important stuff first, and how to write with brevity. He also knew how to instill those high expectations in others, and he always tempered them with patience.

During my first month, I covered a school-board meeting and submitted a story that was, I think, six type-written pages long, double-spaced. Soon after, he dropped it on my desk, and it looked like Collins had cut himself while editing it. His red pencil was merciless. Commas were wrong, sentences were way too long, and needless information was included. At the top, he wrote, "Yank, cut this in half, and don't leave anything important out."

Dr. Seuss

One day, Collins came bounding out of his office to share this from Dr. Seuss:

It has often been said
there's so much to be read,
you never can cram
all those words in your head.

So the writer who breeds
more words than he needs
is making a chore
for the reader who reads.

Later, when I made the move from reporting to editing at other newspapers, that Dr. Seuss mantra framed my approach to editing copy. At one newspaper, reporters called me the Butcher. I chased wasted words without mercy.

It was while I was in Fayetteville that I had the chance to cover perhaps a dozen stories with Nate Caldwell, a legendary Pulitzer Prize–winning reporter at the *Nashville Tennessean*. Nate reminded me of a line from a Gwendolyn Brooks's poem about Robert Frost: "There was a little lightning in his eyes."

I learned the basics from Joe Collins. From Nate Caldwell, I learned subtlety and the importance of thinking through the questions you were going to ask before you asked them. He also never tired of stressing the importance of listening and observation. More than once, I heard him say, "God gave us two ears, two eyes, and one mouth—for a reason."

We were covering a Tennessee Valley Authority (TVA) public hearing on whether a new dam should be built. When it came time for Q & A, reporters asked stock questions and got stock public-relations answers. Then Nate rose and asked if he might pose a question (Nate was polite, southern polite). His question was, "How many months or years will it take this dam to generate the energy to replace the energy that took to build it?" There was dead silence from the TVA guys. If my memory serves, he never got an answer. The Tims Ford Dam, however, did get built.

One of Nate's favorite ripostes about writing came from architect Frank Lloyd Wright: "I'm in favor of keeping dangerous weapons out of the hands of fools. Let's start with typewriters."

Two of my favorite characters in journalism were Bootie Brawley and Heath Thomas, each of whom spent a lifetime in the Salisbury, North Carolina, newsroom. Bootie taught me how to run the wire desk and instilled in me the importance of finding the "Hey Martha" story for page 1. ("Hey Martha" stories are those that the reader was not expecting to find on the front page

Heath Thomas

of the newspaper.) Heath taught me how to report without fear or favor. My favorite story about these two occurred during the centennial celebration of the Civil War, or, as it is still known in parts of the South, the War of Northern Aggression. It seems Bootie and Heath decided to participate in a weekend reenactment at the Gettysburg battlefield. They donned their North Carolina uniforms and headed north. Come Monday, neither Bootie nor Heath reported to work. Ditto Tuesday and beyond. Finally, the publisher's phone rang. A farmer near Gettysburg was calling.

"Do you know a Major Bootie Brawley and Corporal Heath Thomas of the North Carolina Fifth Calvary?"

The publisher, Jimmy Hurley, said he did. "Are they all right?" he inquired.

"They sure are. They've been living in my barn for the better part of a week now. But you better come get them, since they aren't fit to drive."

Jimmy went and picked them up, paid them for the week they had missed, and held no grudges.

During this era, Heath had infiltrated the Ku Klux Klan; he had developed a source inside the group. The Klan would meet, and the next day, the newspaper would report on the meeting. Heath even uncovered a photograph of the county sheriff leading a Klan parade, which was published on page 1.

One day an angry man, armed with a pistol, stormed into the newsroom. "I want Heath Thomas, and I want him now!" he shouted, as most of us dived under our desks.

It turns out he was the grand dragon of the North Carolina KKK. Heath cracked the door to his office, told the guy to take a hike (in coarser language), and asked the photographer to capture the scene so that he could publish it the next day. Finally, the publisher (again Jimmy Hurley) came in and defused the situation. That photo was published the next day.

Bootie was the one who told me the following story about Zebulon Vance, a North Carolina governor and US senator, which Bootie claimed really happened. I've been unable to find proof.

Sometime after the Civil War, the Senate was debating whether to repair bridges in the South destroyed in the conflict. A South Carolina senator was pushing for a bridge over a river near Columbia.

Vance rose in indignation and told his colleagues, "We don't need that bridge. Hell, I can piss halfway across that river."

Someone shouted at Vance, "Sir, you are out of order."

Vance replied, "Hell, yes, I am. If I wasn't, I could piss all the way across that river."

True? Who knows? Who cares? As someone once said in jest, "Don't let the facts get in the way of a good story."

Kindness

CHARLIE, JOHN, AND I PICKED our parents very, very well.

We grew up in the House of Kindness in Pelham Manor, New York. That house shaped us in immeasurable ways.

There was an utter absence of yelling, anger, or unkind words in our home. When I screwed up, Mom would say, "Let's wait until your Dad gets home." (They did parenting things as a team, God bless them.)

When Dad learned of my latest transgression, he'd lower his reading glasses and say something like, "Joseph, I am disappointed in your behavior." Never once, in my memory at least, was I criticized for being who I was. It was always about behavior, and that consistency reinforced the unconditional love our parents had for us.

They also helped shape my future because both were newspaper addicts. We had the *New York Herald Tribune*, the *New York Times,* and the New Rochelle Standard-Star delivered every day. And Dad usually came home with the *New York Daily News.*

I learned an enormous lesson from Dad when, in the ninth grade, my friends started going to private schools: Andover, Exeter, Loomis, and the like. Me too, me too, I begged my parents. The answer was an unequivocal no. It wasn't that they couldn't afford it. They could. But the reason was this: Dad was the product of a private prep school, and he told me that in private school, 1962 would be just like 1925, which was when he had started at the Hill School in

Pottstown, Pennsylvania. Prep school would be boys only, white boys only, and 95 percent Protestant, the rest Catholic. No Jews. Dad contended that public school provided a better opportunity for maturity and learning to live with others: girls, people of many faiths, and people of different colors. Our high school was not overly diverse, but it was diverse.

Charles and Betty Junod

Dad lived by a code and expected the three of us to adhere to the same: tell the truth—whatever the consequences—love your family and friends more than you love yourself, shine your shoes, clean your nails, comb your hair, look people in the eye, shake hands firmly, and, most of all, embrace life with gusto.

When our parents bought their first car, a 1939 blue two-door Chevrolet, they nicknamed it the Bluebird of Happiness. Why not? They were newlyweds, and they had saved Dad's pocket change for a year or so to afford the $900 cost.

As I entered adulthood, we lost Dad. Over time I came to see Mom as the Bluebird of Happiness. Kindness radiated from her. She had a smile for everyone and a reassuring word for folks who were troubled or sad. I've never met another person in whom the kindness gene, if there is such a thing, was so clearly expressed She was a great person, not for any single achievement but for the kindnesses she brought to so many people.

Mind you, she was no patsy. When I was playing golf with her when I was about ten, I hit a bad shot and threw the club. I was warned, "If you do that again, there will be no golf for a year." A couple of holes later, I threw another club. She was a woman of her word. The next time I played golf was 365 days later. Even an appeal to Dad went nowhere.

Let's give the final word on kindness to two novelists.

James M. Barrie, author of *Peter Pan*, advised, "Be kinder than necessary." An unknown writer later added, "For everyone you meet is fighting some kind of battle."

Henry James, author of *The Turn of the Screw*, *The Bostonians*, and many other novels, contended, "Three things in human life are important. The first is to be kind. The second is to be kind. And the third is to be kind."

It really is that simple.

Leadership

_⟶⟶_

PETER DRUCKER ONCE REMARKED, IN a speech I attended, something like this: we know nothing about leadership, so all we do is write books about it.

In conducting quality and customer-service workshops around the country at our company's newspapers, I would ask groups of employees to raise their hands if they've had a great boss. Most folks would raise their hands. I would then ask if they've ever had a terrible boss. Again, most hands would be raised. This was a universal experience at hundreds of training sessions.

Peter Drucker

I would then ask them to describe each boss, and I would write down their descriptions on a flip chart. Over time, I came to realize that every time I did this exercise, the descriptions were mostly the same. The answers in Sioux Falls were essentially the same as answers in Detroit or Fort Myers.

In most every case, employees described a great boss as an engaging, professional, honest, kind, empowering, flexible, and consistent. Such a boss is a good listener who praises in public and criticizes in private, admits mistakes, plays no favorites, thinks things through, and so on.

Likewise, they agreed on what makes a bad boss: a backstabbing, meanspirited, neurotic, inconsistent, egomaniacal, apple-polishing emotional bully who plays favorites, screams, plays people off one another, sucks up, stomps down, and so on.

Then I would ask, "What's common about those descriptions?" Folks would get it. Their descriptions were emotional words, words about behaviors and relationships. Only rarely would someone refer to a boss's skills. No one would say that the boss was a great editor or a bad sales rep.

My conclusion is this. Employees judge managers and leaders on their attitudes and relationships, not on their aptitudes and skills.

A 2009 survey by Harris Interactive found that 28 percent of American workers would fire their boss if they could. In addition, the survey reported that 53 percent of workers did not think their boss was honest, fair, or patient. And 89 percent of workers said their boss was an important factor in their job satisfaction.

One of my favorite authors is Pat Conroy. In *My Losing Season,* he writes of a basketball practice at The Citadel called by the coach on Christmas Day: "What my team needed was coaching and teaching and praise; what my team received once more was contemptuousness, rage, and abuse."

Pat Conroy

How many times have we all seen or experienced what Conroy describes? I'll share just one example. A manager in our company was promoted to a larger operation, and his staff at the smaller operation sent the colleagues at the bigger place a dozen black roses. Why? This manager would, on a Friday afternoon, call a staff meeting for the next day (Saturday, a day off for this particular discipline), and *he would not show up.* What do you think? I guess he was showing his staff just how powerful he was. And what did the company do? It promoted him to another operation where he was the boss. Under his "leadership," the newspaper was decimated in people, morale, content, and revenue. Go figure.

We've all seen—and worked for—people who were promoted beyond their skill and attitude sets (the Peter principle). While working in Fort Myers, I came to know a fine reporter named Lee Melsek. He could have worked anywhere, for much bigger money; Lee was that good. But Fort Myers was home, and home he would stay. A diligent, thoughtful grinder of the highest order, he was so good that management promoted him to assistant metro editor, a job in which he did not do well.

All the attributes that made him a superb reporter—impatience, drive, and working alone—were all wrong for an editor, whose job it was to nurture younger reporters. Lee expected any story that he edited to be as good as if he had written it. Whoa. There were lots of tears. Lee and management both quickly realized this was not a good move, and Lee went back to reporting (at his editor's salary—smart management) and shining light in dark places for many more years.

Motivation

THIS IS, I BELIEVE, A widely misunderstood word.

Too many people—in sports, business, schools, and so on—believe that motivation is an external force that propels an individual toward a goal.

"Boy, the Yankees' manager sure knows how to motivate his players."

"That teacher motivates me to study harder."

"Your boss can really motivate the staff."

Nope.

The dictionary defines motivation in two ways:

1. The reason or reasons one has for acting or behaving in a particular way.
2. The general desire or willingness of someone to do something.

If they are effective leaders, the manager, the teacher, and the boss all do the same thing in different ways. They create positive workplace environments where folks come in motivated to excel. They give their players, students, and employees room to grow in their jobs through training, self-learning, and experience.

The only person who can motivate me is me. The degree of motivation is linked to the environment of the workplace or classroom.

Ineffective leaders either ignore workplace environments or create dispirited or meanspirited environments.

I don't believe that there is a formula for what makes a great workplace environment. That depends on the personalities and the type of work. A positive environment on a Texas oil rig is going to be very different than a positive environment an East Coast boarding school.

Having survived and studied my share of nasty managers, I decided they probably all shared two traits: they are insecure, and they are bullies.

Sally Jenkins

Sportswriter Sally Jenkins, writing in the *Washington Post* about the NFL's Washington Redskins' poor 2009 season, commented, "Why do the Redskins continually make the same management mistakes? One possible answer is they suffer from something called 'toxic management.' Denial and refusal to accept criticism are classic hallmarks of it, and so is shifting blame to others."

Toxic management is not just a term; it's a pathology, and experts have written books about it. A leader in the field is Roy Lubit, a member of the faculty of the Mount Sinai School of Medicine in New York and the author of *Coping with Toxic Managers and Subordinates*. According to Lubit, toxic managers are "rigid, aggressive, self-centered. They're also divisive…Toxic managers actually prefer tension to stability, because it's a demonstration of their personal power."

While job hunting, I was given some good advice. Once you understand who your direct manager will be if hired, ask employees who are also direct reports what kind of manager he or she is.

Neighborliness

_⌒_

A MEMBER OF MY CHURCH, Edd Houck, a former Virginia state senator, was asked by the parish to present an award to an organization that provides day care to disabled adults. Our church provides them space during the day.

Edd cited Jesus's admonition of the two greatest commandments: love thy God with all thy heart, and love thy neighbor as thyself.

But Houck edited Jesus's words! Houck's version was this: Love thy God with all thy heart...without an asterisk. Love thy neighbor as thyself...without an asterisk.

Brazen? Sure.

Insightful? Yes.

Understanding of human nature? Absolutely.

Houck's message that day spoke volumes about how we profess to love God and love our neighbors, with exceptions. We all have exceptions, and that's what makes us sinners.

Houck grew up in a Virginia that was the last bastion of resistance to integration in the United States. The segregationists called it "massive

Edd Houck

resistance," and it was led, shamefully, by the editor of the largest newspaper in the state.

But I am sure that experience informed not only Houck's politics but, more importantly, his world view.

At the ceremony, there were about a dozen or so adults with startling disabilities, and Houck reminded us that they are God's creatures, too, and that they are beloved by him.

That day Houck provided a rich and important lesson on how one might fulfill Christ's admonitions and live a more righteous life.

Openness

WHILE WORKING IN FLORIDA, I interviewed the owner of a furniture-man-ufacturing operation. He was opening a new factory.

This man was the stereotypical Bubba. He lacked what the elites might call "polish." What he didn't lack were smarts and a deep understanding of what motivates folks in the workplace.

How did I reach that conclusion? On every wall of the new building (including the restrooms) were posters with the same message:

> Every rule in
> this company
> can be challenged—
> except this one.

I don't suspect he invented the idea, but people pay big, big money for management consultants and management training. And here was Bubba trumping the field with eleven words.

Here are some questions to ask yourself:

* Do you think Bubba's employees went the extra mile for him?
* Do you think employee turnover was a problem?
* Do you think absenteeism was a problem?
* Do you think Bubba was successful?

Bubba and other business leaders who practice openness with employees and staff are more likely to succeed than those who are secretive, reclusive, or dictatorial.

A story is told about Herb Kelleher, founder of Southwest Airlines. It seems that a banker friend of his was having a morale problem with his staff. He asked Herb to speak with his senior executives about it. They arrived at the bank and made their way from the parking lot to the executive offices for the meeting. Herb stopped at the door to the meeting room and told his friend that he didn't need to talk with senior managers because he already knew the source of the problem.

The banker asked how Herb could know what was wrong, not having met the executives.

The problem, Herb told his friend, is you. On their way to the meeting room, they had walked past several dozen of the bank's employees, and the bank president had failed to say "good morning" to any of them.

Patriotism

Now here is a loaded word, at least to some in my generation.

In the 1960s, mainstream patriotism was summed up in bumper stickers that said things like "My country, right or wrong" and "America: Love it or leave it."

These "patriots" supported the Vietnam War through thick and thin while some fifty-nine thousand Americans perished in what is now pretty much viewed as a colossal act of political hubris and military stupidity.

The hypocrisy of these sunshine patriots found full flower forty years later in one Dick Cheney, the former vice president who pushed the president into a useless Iraqi war. During the Vietnam War, Cheney received five student deferments. Some years later, he was asked why he had sought so many outs. "I had better things to do," he reportedly said. What a prince of a guy.

At the beginning of the second Gulf War after September eleven, sunshine patriotism surfaced again. Bumper stickers supporting the troops were everywhere, and the airwaves were full of bombastic blather about uniting against a common enemy. Yet most Americans had no skin in the game. The only people who did were the soldiers, marines, and their families. Our family is especially blessed because our son and our nephew survived numerous combat tours.

I had a bumper sticker on my car that read,

America is not at war.
America's military is at war.
America is at the mall.

I can't tell you how many versions of "Right on" I got from folks who read that message.

The military should not do this stuff alone. Both George W. Bush and Barack Obama failed to recognize that fact. Imagine what a fifty-cent national-gas-tax increase would have done for care of the wounded. But nobody in leadership stood up in either administration. What a shame. The unfortunate message from Bush and Obama was this: leadership goes to war (without just cause in the case of Iraq), sustains it, and soldiers and marines—and their families—are the only ones who pay the price. The rest of America goes about its business.

Quality of Life

My wife, Marilyn Greene, spent the better part of three decades covering the world as a journalist and, later, as a free-press advocate. Her experiences were rich and sometimes dangerous (Somalia, the first Gulf War, and Haiti) and always educational.

Marilyn Greene

I learned an immensely important lesson from her, one that I still sometimes forget.

Marilyn would return from some hellhole, and she would say, "We have no idea how lucky we are to live in the United States."

Most of the world's peoples live in poverty, without health care, schools, and good water.

We Americans often take all that for granted. We (including me) forget that we are smothered with abundance, unlike any other people on Earth. Yet we seem to think we live in a time of scarcity.

I have seen mind-numbing need firsthand only once. My wife was teaching journalism in Cameroon for three months, and I went to visit. For someone raised in the relative luxury of Westchester County, New York, to call that experience an eye-opener would be an understatement of the highest order. It was poverty as I've never seen it. There were open, filthy sewers, people bathing in filthy streams, and a life expectancy of fortysomething. Four people she taught or worked with died of disease within two years; they were all young or middle aged.

One Sunday we went to church, a big Presbyterian church in Douala, the largest city in the country. There were a thousand people, easy, on three levels. We were the only white folks in the church. On the way in, we were asked to sign the guest book. We did. Sometime into the service, the preacher asked all visitors to stand up. A dozen or so of us did. The entire place burst into song:

> We are so glad you are here,
> We are so glad you are here,
> God bless you, God bless you.
> We are so glad you are here.

It was the most moving church moment of my life. Would that more American churches would make visitors feel that way.

What I witnessed—and learned—during that three-hour service was this: people in very tough situations can exude a joy that no burden can extinguish.

Here's a thought I wish I'd had when raising our boys. Parents with children over thirteen, some summer don't take your kids to Disney World or some beach resort. Take them to Mozambique or the Philippines, to any African nation or some poor place in America. They will probably hate the "vacation," but I'll bet that when they are adults, they will thank you for it. I believe the journey will change their world view and change their lives.

Consider this from www.globalrichlist.com. If you earn $50,000 a year, you are in the top 1 percent of the richest people on Earth. With the world's population at seven billion, the website estimated that you earn more money than 6.9 billion of your fellow human beings.

In 2013 I spent two weeks at St. George's College in Jerusalem, taking a course entitled The Palestine of Jesus. We visited all the important Old and New Testament sites. It was the most rewarding two weeks of my life, partially because I learned this prayer from an Australian named John Stuart, who was our chaplain: "We ask that our privilege not be kept to ourselves but shared outwardly as a sign of God's hospitality to all the world."

It is a prayer that haunts me.

Retention

I SPENT A PORTION OF my later career working with newspapers on improving quality and customer service. With lots of input from many smart folks, I conjured up this formula for success in service:

Respect + Response + Reliability + Recovery = Retention
Respect your customers in all things.
Respond to your customers quickly. Not in twenty-four hours. The same day. Tons of research indicates that a customer ignored is a customer lost.
Be reliable. Do what you say you are going to do.
Recover effectively when you or your organization makes a mistake. Don't hide behind policy. Apologize, and take care of the mistake immediately.

In the newspaper business, we have three distinct external customers: readers, subscribers, and advertisers. Each has its own needs and demands, and smart media executives figure out how to satisfy those needs and demands on a regular basis.

For most businesses, improving customer retention is an important key to improving the bottom line. That is certainly true in the newspaper business.

Now that I am out on my own, retention has taken on a broader meaning for me. Each of us is a vessel that retains many things.

Retention is a key part of our character, our nature, and our personality.

We retain different things, for different lengths of time.

Some of us retain *lots* of things. See the TV program *Hoarders* for examples. Others of us retain very few things. See the Jesuits.

We retain memories. Some great. Some good. Some warm. Some bad. Some cold.

We retain money…at least some of us do.

We retain friendships, passions, enemies, thoughts, ideas, and love.

What we retain is who we are and who we become.

Stewardship

WHEN I FIRST ENCOUNTERED THE concept of stewardship, I understood it to be the collection of money from the faithful in a congregation in order to keep the lights on and the preacher paid (however little it was, and it usually was little. Still is.)

But over the years, I've come to believe that we all are born stewards—of the Earth in all its richness. It is one more gift from God. William Barclay, a twentieth-century Scottish theologian, wrote, "For Jesus, the whole wide world was the garment of the living God." It is for each one of us to decide whether we are active stewards or inactive stewards. I came late to active stewardship, but I am glad I am finally arriving.

In my church, we strive to fulfill the three T's of stewardship: giving of our time, our talent, and our treasure. We also strive to tithe: to give 10 percent of our gross income. But, as a group, we fail miserably. Our national church estimates that we give about 2 percent of our gross income, on average.

Too often, we approach giving from a position of scarcity rather than abundance.

Stephen Covey got it right when he wrote, "People with a scarcity mentality tend to see everything terms of win-lose. There is only so much, and if someone else has it, that means there will be less for me." He added, "The more principle-centered we become, the more we develop an abundance mentality." If you believe, as I do, that all you are and all you have is from God, can it be so difficult to return 10 percent to him? Can you live on the other 90 percent? A few years ago, I read about a family that divvied up its income

Stephen Covey

this way. It gives 10 percent to the church, saves 10 percent, has fun with 10 percent, and lives off the remaining 70 percent. That is so smart.

And here's more information from www.globalrichlist.com:

- Eight dollars could buy you fifteen organic apples *or* twenty-five fruit trees for farmers in Honduras to grow and sell fruit at their local market.
- Thirty dollars could buy you a DVD box set *or* a first-aid kit for a whole village in Haiti.
- Seventy-three dollars could buy you a new mobile phone *or* a new mobile health clinic to care for AIDS orphans in Uganda.
- And $2,400 could buy you a monster high-definition television *or* schooling for an entire generation of school children in an Angolan village.

Choices. Life is nothing more than choices.

Jimmy Hurley, my old boss in North Carolina, was a great giver. He was wealthy, and he and his wife, Gerry, used that wealth to improve the lives of their neighbors, many of their neighbors. At his death, a longtime colleague wrote, "As publisher, Hurley followed his father's example of investing in equipment, being efficient, preserving cash flow, and creating stability. But he also sought to improve employee pay, advertising rates, circulation numbers, and the paper's overall appearance."

The colleague quoted Hurley on his philosophy: "On family newspapers, I think too many families try to make a good living without working. I think our generation was very lucky we didn't grow up feeling rich. We grew up feeling an opportunity to contribute."

During and after Jimmy's days at the *Post*, the Hurleys led some of the community's biggest fundraising campaigns and contributed millions to projects that helped to build parks, YMCAs, homeless shelters, college buildings, scholarships, senior centers, libraries, swimming pools, school athletic facilities, and more.

"I lean on people," he said. "I know who has the money. They can't poor-mouth me."

But the always-competitive Hurley said that he never took on a fundraising cause he didn't believe in or one in which he couldn't be a winner.

"I never talked anybody into giving money," Hurley explained. "I give them a chance to invest their profits in this community."

Out of the public eye, Hurley quietly funded college students who needed financial assistance, employees who could use help with medical or utility bills, and residents who required a leg up.

I went on several fundraising calls with Hurley when I worked at his newspaper. My favorite was this one. He was leading an effort to build a community pool in a poor section of town, where mostly black people lived. We visited a very rich man who said he'd be glad to contribute. He wrote a check and handed it to Hurley. Hurley looked at the number, looked at the guy, and said something like, "This is an embarrassment. Keep your miserly cash." The check was for a pittance. And we walked out, with Hurley muttering and cursing. I believe that the next day a much larger check arrived at the newspaper for the pool.

Hurley spoke about the legacy he hoped to leave.

"When the Great Scorer comes to mark against my name," he said, "he's going to ask what happened to all those opportunities he entrusted me with. I don't want to have to tell him, 'I hid 'em in a lockbox at the bank.'"

What a great lesson in stewardship. It's not how much—for most of us cannot give what Jimmy and Gerry gave. Rather, it is a matter of proportion. What percentage of your financial being (and your soul) are you willing to give away to help others who have less than you?

Trust and Teamwork

IN THE EARLY 1980s, I was lucky enough to operate in an environment that engendered trust, presumed teamwork, and, as a result, produced excellent results.

When I left a Florida job in the late 1970s, for a job at a "small" Upstate New York newspaper, little did I know I was about to enter a newsroom bubbling over with potential, energy, wide-ranging talent, and naked ambition. It was love at first sight...not only with the whole Ithaca newsroom but with the woman who, on a miraculous 1981 August night overlooking Cayuga Lake, agreed to marry me. In a flash, I was wedded and the stepfather of three marvelous young men.

In our newsroom, there were obstacles to overcome, and they were overcome. I was management, and there was a union. Still, despite the occasional flare-up, the news team operated at a furious and glorious pace.

Helping fuel that pace was a disheveled kid from Long Island who wore black sneakers, smoked Camel filters nonstop, and, as I learned in about a day, had the best nose for news I had ever met. Promoting him to city editor at, I think, age twenty-three was one of my best decisions ever. Phil Lerman went on to a fine career as executive director of *America's Most Wanted*. His nose for news never wavered when he flipped to television.

Earlier, I placed the word "small" in quotation marks. As newspapers go, the *Ithaca Journal* was small—in staff, in circulation, and in advertising revenue—compared with our sister newspapers in places like Rochester, New York, and Cincinnati. When our newspaper was selected as the best newspaper in the ninety-plus-newspaper Gannett chain for the year 1981, we were all stunned and proceeded to get gloriously drunk. The entire staff—several dozen men and women—had contributed journalistically to our award-winning paper. Many of us, I think, learned some important lessons from the experience:

Phil Lerman

- Define a mission and drive relentlessly toward it.
- Expect excellence, and understand failure to perform at a high level every day.
- Honor—and reward—independent thinking.
- Give folks room to let their egos run, at least for a while. (I remember watching an editor standing between a headstrong reporter and a stubborn photographer as she tried to negotiate the fair-minded balance of words and photographs on a story that had to fit on one page. The solution, amazingly, satisfied both parties, and I left the room chuckling.)
- Enjoy the success, and then buckle down and do better. (The next year we were runner-up as best newspaper; it was a disappointment but, in another view, a victory for consistent excellence.)

The gang, naturally, broke up, and most of us went on to other journalism careers, mostly at larger organizations. But we never forgot those days. We never will.

Understanding

_____⌒

PERHAPS THE RICHEST AND MOST formative experiences for me were the five summers I worked at a Jewish beach club, the Eldorado Shore and Yacht Club, on Long Island Sound. There was a shore but no yachts. This was a social club.

Over those years, I worked as busboy, waiter, and, best of all, cabana boy.

For a sheltered gentile, the Eldo opened up an exciting world previously unknown to me. I am not alone. I am pretty sure that many of us who experienced the Eldo are more tolerant and understanding of different cultures, religions, and personalities than we were before.

The Eldo welcomed as members Jews of all nationalities, unlike other Jewish clubs that discriminated based on nationality. But the Eldo did discriminate! Gentiles were welcome but only as employees. We gentiles could not have cared less, for the club was filled with life, laughter, and learning—and good money to earn.

Especially revered were members we called the Numbered Ones—those who had survived the Nazi camps.

I knew one man, blinded in the camps, who had a driver named Ivan the Terrible and a dog named God Bless America. After I helped him move into his cabana, he said he wanted to tip me twenty dollars. He pulled out a roll of cash and peeled off a fifty-dollar bill. I looked at the fifty, looked at the blind man, and made the right decision. I told him he was handing me a fifty, not a twenty. He said, "I know; I was testing you." (It turned that out his driver every morning arranged his roll of cash in exactly the same order so that the man knew what bill he was pulling from the roll.)

One woman had arrived from Poland at age fifteen and had never seen a toothbrush. After we became close, I asked her, "How rich are you?"

She replied, "Joey, my bank, they don't count my money anymore. They weigh it." Her laughter crossed the sound.

Folks like these taught me four big lessons:

1. Tolerance is vital to social order; don't abuse it.
2. Life can and will be hard. Lean on your faith.
3. Humor and laughter make the world a better place.
4. If you are full of yourself, you are full of you-know-what.

Self-determination is a wondrous trait. I do not remember one person at the club who worked for a corporation or for someone else. The place was filled with entrepreneurs: dentists, liquor store owners, car dealers, lawyers, and doctors. They were folks who ran their own lives, on their own terms. There was even a bookie. He had three telephones in his cabana with direct lines to the New York tracks!

I learned the essence of capitalism from a gentleman named Mickey Lipp, a car dealer in The Bronx. One summer after I had been named head cabana boy, I was lucky enough to serve the men's poker game for the summer. Ten men played six days a week, all day long, nothing but five-card stud. I was responsible for keeping them supplied with water, food (bagels and lox were the table favorite), and three fresh decks of cards every day. I bought the cards for $2.50 a deck at the club office and got reimbursed by the players. Mickey pulled me aside early in the summer (he did not play) and advised me that a nearby department store sold the same decks for ninety-nine cents each. Buy them there, he said, and then sell them to the men at the regular price of $2.50. In 1968 that was a nice margin—eighteen decks a week for the summer, with a profit of $1.51 per deck. I wised up fast, thanks to Mickey.

Mickey said with a wink, "Buy low; sell high. Live life."

Well, I've tried.

Volunteering

IF ENTERPRISE AND HARD WORK built this nation, volunteering plays a major role in sustaining it.

What hospital could function normally without volunteers?
What church could survive without volunteers?
What food pantry could operate without volunteers?
Consider these numbers:

- The US volunteer rate was little changed at 25.3 percent for the year ending in September 2014, the US Bureau of Labor Statistics reports. About 62.8 million people volunteered through or for an organization at least once between September 2013 and September 2014. The volunteer rate in 2013 was 25.4 percent.
- The volunteer rates for both men and women (22.0 percent and 28.3 percent, respectively) were little changed. Women continued to volunteer at a higher rate than men, across all age groups, educational levels, and other major demographic characteristics.
- By age, thirty-five- to forty-four-year-olds were most likely to volunteer (29.8 percent). For persons forty-five years and over, the volunteer rate tapered off as age increased.

My wife and I volunteer at our church's thrift shop—a two-story house on church property with eight rooms filled with furniture, clothes, tools, and toys.

The shop's primary focus is to help folks in need. Prices are low. When we know someone is hurting, we make the sure the cash register doesn't ring.

One story will suffice to illustrate why volunteering can be so personally and spiritually rewarding. Weeks before a recent Christmas, I was working the cash register. A woman came in. She had bruises on her face. Her husband, she said, had just kicked her and the children out of the house. The children were waiting in a friend's van as their mother came in to shop. They were headed to the shelter for battered women in town.

She said, "I have eight dollars and nothing for Christmas for the kids. And no winter coats."

Another volunteer heard this and took the woman upstairs, where the clothes and toys were located.

When the woman left about an hour later, we loaded six large garbage bags filled with clothes, coats, and toys.

The woman left with her eight dollars intact.

Willpower

THE DICTIONARY OFFERS NUMEROUS DEFINITIONS of "will" and "willpower."

Permit me to add another. Actually, it's a synonym. If you looked up the word "willpower" in *my* dictionary, you would encounter a picture of Allen H. Neuharth, a man who personified the word.

Ah, I pity most of you who never had the pleasure (and sometimes pain) of knowing Al, not to mention working for him.

Al Neuharth was CEO and chairman, in the 1970s and 1980s, of Gannett. He was a force of nature—a poor kid from the wilds of South Dakota who rose to run the largest media company (at the time) on earth.

Al Neuharth

A bigger pain in the ass, I have never met. And I say that with affection.

It was my good fortune to hang around Al in the mid-1980s, as he was winding down his career. As he neared retirement, I asked him what he would miss the most about being CEO. Without missing a beat, he said, "My jets." He had, at that time, not been on a commercial airliner in twenty-five years.

Al lived large.

It would be easy to share many Al stories, but here's what is cemented in my mind. Al said something like this to his senior staff: "Let's join the big leagues and create a national newspaper."

Inside the company, the naysayers went wild—mostly the finance types. Al stared them down. *USA Today* debuted on September 15, 1982. In attendance at the debut party was President Ronald Reagan. Al dreamed no small dreams.

For years, *USA Today* bled red ink and sucked up resources from the company's other ninety-plus newspapers. The finance types repeatedly sought to kill the newspaper. With his force of will, coupled with tactics that would make Machiavelli proud, Al beat back, beat down, and beat up his internal opposition. The external ridicule was immediate and continued for years; witness the moniker "McPaper." Rather than be cowed by that label, Al reveled in it and marketed it. Al was a marketing savant.

When the newspaper debuted, Warren Buffett said publicly he'd eat crow if *USA Today* ever made a profit.

When the profit arrived, Neuharth told me to call Buffett to ask where we should deliver the crow.

Buffett howled his congratulations.

But Neuharth was no saint. When he was traveling the country on what was called "Buscapade," a bus tour to visit all fifty states and interview all fifty governors (that is, we rode the bus across the country; Al rode his jet to meet us in state capitals), he decided in Indiana he wanted to see *Hoosiers*, a movie that had just been released only in Los Angeles and New York.

"Get me a copy of it so that I can watch it tomorrow night in some theater," he demanded.

"Al," several of us replied, "that's impossible."

His response went something like this: "Get me the goddamned movie or get another job." Clarity was one of Al's strong suits. We got the movie.

Xtra

‿๑

FOR ALL FOLKS WHO WRITE for a living or a hobby, here, for me, are two memorable pieces of writing—my extras for this publication.

The musical *South Pacific* debuted in 1949, a time of Jim Crow laws, segregated schools, and bans on interracial marriage. Along came James Michener, Richard Rogers, and Oscar Hammerstein with a book and then a musical set during World War II.

Rogers and Hammerstein

Not only was there one interracial love story, there were two! It was staged in 1949 in America, for Pete's sake. And Joe Cable, the marine in turmoil over his relationship with an island girl, sings this song (words by Hammerstein):

You've got to be taught
To hate and fear,
You've got to be taught
From year to year,
It's got to be drummed
In your dear little ear
You've got to be carefully taught.

You've got to be taught to be afraid
Of people whose eyes are oddly made,
And people whose skin is a diff'rent shade,
You've got to be carefully taught.

You've got to be taught before it's too late,
Before you are six or seven or eight,
To hate all the people your relatives hate,
You've got to be carefully taught!

What's fascinating about Brooks Atkinson's April 8, 1949, review in the *New York Times* of opening night is the absence of any mention of this song or of the interracial relationships. (Atkinson loved the show, but he missed the news.)

Great writing can cause discomfort. I'll bet lots of folks were squirming when they first heard this song. Do you think this little song had anything to do with sparking the revolution that would start a few years hence? Anything at all? Musicals are sometimes mocked as theatrical fluff. If this is fluff, give me more of it.

My favorite passage about the craft of writing comes from William Faulkner's Nobel Prize speech:

William Faulkner

I decline to accept the end of man. It is easy enough to say that man is immortal simply because he will endure: that when the last dingdong of doom has clanged and faded from the last worthless rock hanging tideless in the last red and dying evening, that even then there will still be one more sound: that of his puny inexhaustible voice, still talking.

I refuse to accept this. I believe that man will not merely endure: he will prevail. He is immortal, not because he alone among creatures has an inexhaustible voice, but because he has a soul, a spirit capable of compassion and sacrifice and endurance. The poet's, the writer's, duty is to write about these things. It is his privilege to help man endure by lifting his heart, by reminding him of the courage and honor and hope and pride and compassion and pity and sacrifice which have been the glory of his past. The poet's voice need not merely be the record of man, it can be one of the props, the pillars to help him endure and prevail.

Yes

_⸱_

SOME YEARS BACK, I VISITED one of Gannett's newspapers. Walking into the lobby, I was startled to see this poster plastered everywhere:

What part of NO
don't you understand?

Now that is a simply stupid message for customers and employees alike. I challenged the executive team to strip the posters and come up with a message that was more procustomer. Their solution:

What part of YES
may I help you with?

That new message was the catalyst for the newspaper's management to place a far greater emphasis on creating a positive environment for customers and employees alike.

Zest

_6

WHENEVER I ENCOUNTER THE WORD "zest," I see a face—the face of Garland Gaither of Salisbury, North Carolina. I was privileged to know Garland during the four years I lived in that city in the 1970s. It is difficult to describe him, because he was so much more than the sum of his parts. Let me try.

Garland was a very big man who came in a small, cheerful package. For me, he symbolized many things:

* The value of hard work, especially a willingness to do work that many others would shun as beneath them
* Kindness to all he encountered
* Refusal to accept the ways of the past with a stubbornness untainted by victimhood
* A simplicity that disguised just how smart he was

Garland was maybe five foot four inches tall. My favorite image of him was when he picked up his wife from work at

Garland Gaither

79

the Capitol Theater; the two rode home on Garland's old bicycle (Garland claimed his bike was more than fifty years old), his wife sitting on the seat while Garland stood on the pedals and pumped.

Garland, who died at age 92 in 2002, started working at the Salisbury Post in the 1934. His job was to light the fires that melted the lead that enabled printers to set the type to produce the newspaper. He was also the custodian. When I came to know him, the linotype machines were gone, but Garland and his six carrier boys were still delivering 600 newspapers to his neighborhood, the black section of Salisbury. If Garland was your carrier, you got your newspaper every afternoon, and every week you paid your bill, plus an extra ten cents for having the privilege of Mr. Garland Gaither himself deliver your newspaper.

He would also hawk newspapers on a street corner. I can still hear his shout: "Get your *Salisbury* right here."

And here's the thing. Starting as a boy, Garland went to the bank most every day it was open to deposit the money he had earned. Some years before I knew him, he discovered stockbrokers, and, well, you get the idea.

Here was a black man who was born into the Jim Crow South, where most avenues of success were closed to him. Yet he carved out his own route to happiness and financial security, always with a smile on his face and a hello for everyone. He washed windows and cleaned bathrooms late at night in the downtown business district. Garland was a man of stature and substance, a man from whom life lessons could be—and were—learned.

It is fitting that this rumination ends with Garland. May you be blessed enough to have had a Garland Gaither cross your path for a time on your journey.

Even better, may you evoke the spirit of Garland wherever life takes you.

--30--

SPECIAL THANKS TO MY FRIEND and former colleague Carrie Wendell for her help with this manuscript.

Photographs of Jimmy Hurley, Heath Thomas and Garland Gaither courtesy of The Salisbury (NC) Post

Made in the USA
Columbia, SC
25 May 2018